Seth is five, but he can write his name.

Seth is five, but he can write his name.

He drops his name in a box
at the store.

He drops his name in a box
at the store.

Seth's big wish is to win a blue bike.

Seth's big wish is to win a
blue bike.

If the man picks his name, he will win.

If the man picks his name,
he will win.

At home he waits to hear the phone ring.

At home he waits to hear
the phone ring.

His dad will teach him to ride and to use the brakes.

His dad will teach him to
ride and to use the brakes.

Chip, his dog, will chase him.

Chip, his dog, will chase him.

He will whiz past Gram
and wave and grin.

He will whiz past Gram
and wave and grin.

Then Seth will ride with his left hand up.

Then Seth will ride with
his left hand up.

He will be *quite a hot shot.

He will be <u>qu</u>ite a hot shot.

Seth waits and waits in the chair near the phone.

Seth waits and waits in the chair near the phone.

His dream is that the phone will ring.

His dream is that the phone will ring.

"Ring.... ring."

Seth picks up the phone.
"Yes?"

"Ring.... ring."

Seth picks up the phone. "Yes?"

The man tells Seth that he can claim his prize.

The man tells Seth that he can claim his prize.

"Whee! Thanks a lot! It will be such fun."

"Whee! Thanks a lot! It will be such fun."

The End

The End